WRITTEN BY SHAWANDA R. RANDOLPH, MBA, MAT
PUBLISHED BY FRESH MANNA PUBLISHING

ALL RIGHTS RESERVED.

NO PART OF THIS WORK MAY BE REPRODUCED OR TRANSMITTED IN ANY FORM OR BY ANY MEANS, ELECTRONIC OR MECHANICAL, INCLUDING PHOTOCOPYING AND RECORDING, OR BY ANY INFORMATION STORAGE OR RETRIEVAL SYSTEM, EXCEPT AS MAY BE EXPRESSLY PERMITTED BY THE 1976 COPYRIGHT ACT OR IN WRITING FROM THE PUBLISHER. REQUESTS FOR PERMISSION SHOULD BE ADDRESSED BY CONTACTING FRESHMANNA@SHAWANDARANDOLPH.COM

FOR MORE INFORMATION ABOUT THE AUTHOR AND OTHER PRODUCTS VISIT:

WWW.SHAWANDARANDOLPH.COM

   RANDOLPH.SHAWANDA

  @SHAWANDA_RANDOLPH

Welcome!

I am grateful for the opportunity to accompany you on your path of self-exploration!

It's essential not to underestimate the opportunity to understand how to move forward in life by following God. Our perception of ourselves and the One who created us greatly depends on it.

I'm here to assist you in exploring your true God-given identity and uncovering it. By seeking Him and embracing your identity, you'll be able to embrace new opportunities with confidence, clarity, and a sense of purpose. Most importantly, understanding yourself through the eyes of God, your Creator, will strengthen your relationship with Him and increase your faith.

Shawanda R. Randolph

ABOUT ME

Apostolic leader, teacher, and mentor Shawanda R. Randolph has spent over three decades mentoring, developing, and leading young leaders from government, private sectors, and various ministry settings. Studying under the late Bishop Dr. B. Derone Robinson, Apostle has a unique style of teaching that helps the unchurch connect to and understand The Word of God, increasing their desire to seek a deeper relationship with God and find purpose in life according to His Word.

SHAWANDARANDOLPH.COM | LEARNING TO LOVE YOURSELF, AGAIN

SELF COMMITMENT

This will take commitment, dedication, and hard work from you.

Commitment

This is a commitment to self! This is YOUR journey. You will only get out of this what you are willing to put into it. But you must understand that this is YOUR process, and it is for you and you alone. While you may have many goals, you must be properly positioned to receive your heart's desire. Before having a solid connection and commitment with something we desire, we must first be willing to connect and commit to ourselves. This relationship, starts with understanding who we are in God, then forming a proper union with Him. As we learn to partner together in this union, God brings us into the fold to understand how to move to achieve our goals with HIM at the center. Thus you must be committed to discovering your INDIVIDUAL identity to then understand what God wants for your life and why.

Dedication

Devoted to the journey! This is not a race to the finish line, and will take dedication to stay the course. We will have mapped out sessions, but are you willing to stay the course and continue to work on yourself in between? This means following through on readings, journaling, prayer, and other exercises to help facilitate the process. In addition, you must dedicate yourself to following through after our sessions are over. The second half of dedication is staying on task with assignments and appointments. It is important to note that, yes, you have tried many programs or services in the past, BUT the goal is to make this the final time you start something without finishing and getting the results you have long desired.

Hardwork

The willingness and desire to deal with tough issues. It is important to understand that this journey requires the need to dig and uncover potential barriers that have prevented you from achieving your goals in the past. This requires hard work and, at times, difficult conversations, but will prove beneficial as you find yourself. As we have the tough conversations that reveal barriers and strongholds, we become free to move forward in embracing our God-given identity and the purpose and plans God has for us.

PRO MISE

JOURNEY OUTLINE

01 — **SESSION 1 – DEFINING DESIRES**
DEFINING PERSONAL DESIRES AND OVERCOMING SELF-SABOTAGE

06 — **SESSION 2 – ALL ABOUT ME**
REDEFINING IDENTITY AND BUILDING COURAGE AND SELF-WORTH

23 — **SESSION 3 – THE FUTURE YOU**
REDEFINING THE FUTURE AND BUILDING ON GOD-GIVEN DREAMS

32 — **SESSION 4 – A NEW FOUND FAITH**
REDEFINING PERSONAL FAITH AND FINDING CLARITY FOR THE FUTURE

36 — **SESSION 5 – SELF-PRESERVATION**
REDEFINING SELF-CARE AND UNDERSTANDING PIVITOL AXIS POINTS IN LIFE

40 — **SESSION 6 – THE ART OF GRATITUDE**
REDEFINING GRATITUDE AND REBUILDING HEAVENLY RELATIONSHIPS

01
DEFINING DESIRES

GOAL: REMOVE THE "I DON'T KNOWS..."

It's important to delve into the root of your deep desires. What is motivating you to crave them so strongly? This exploration can expose underlying reasons why things may not be going as planned. It can also bring to light any self-sabotaging behaviors you may be engaging in, as well as highlight any actions you may be neglecting to take.

Background:
The thing we want so badly, we often sabotage.

Sometimes, we want something so badly that we end up ruining it. We become overly controlling and try to mold it into the ideal image we have created in our minds. But when reality doesn't match our expectations, we either try even harder to force it or give up hope altogether. We may even start believing in false religions, idols, or beliefs to fill the void.

This fixation on our desires can make it difficult to involve God in the process. We start to believe that we are not worthy of our desires and forget that we need His help to make them happen. It's important to trace our steps to understand how we got to this point and unravel the effects of our actions.

By breaking down our ideal image, we can start to rethink what our perfect life or career should look like. This can help us understand why we may be struggling to achieve our dreams. Remembering to involve God in the process can bring us closer to truly fulfilling our desires in a healthy and fulfilling way.

> "She is clothed with strength and dignity;
> she can laugh at the days to come."
> (Proverbs 31:25)

Reflection Exercise

Instructions:
- Spend time reflecting on each prompt and respond appropriately
- Write complete thoughts and do not leave any space blank
- It is important to schedule time in your day to do the exercise so you are intentional with your time. Recommend placing it on your schedule and setting an alarm to ensure you have adequate time to write and reflect without being disturbed.

Dig Deep!

"For you created my inmost being; you knit me together in my mother's womb."
(Psalm 139:13)

UNDERSTANDING DESIRES

What is the desire and what makes it ideal to you?

Why do you desire this so deeply?

Where this come from?

Who are the role models for what you desire? Why are they the role models? What about them makes them role models?

Explore their personality and behaviors, how they interact with others, how they make others feel, how they resolve matters, how they communicate, and their faith.

If there are no role models then who are the role models of what you do not want, and discuss why they are not ideal. Is this what's driving you to have what you desire?

UNDERSTANDING DESIRES

02

ALL ABOUT ME!
GOAL - SELF-EXPLORATION IS VITAL

It is necessary to introspect and truly understand oneself before forming meaningful connections with others. This introspection enables an individual to comprehend the purpose behind those who enter their lives, especially those brought by a higher power. Above all, this process helps in accepting oneself and establishing higher personal standards and expectations.

All About Me!

Background:
There are two important aspects of our identity we must come to _ _ _ with?

First, who are you? There is the person we wake up to each and every day. The person we introduce to others. This is the person who has hopes and dreams, the person that has accomplished so much and dares to accomplish even greater things. This is also the person who sits and reflects on how life is and could be when alone. Sometimes this person is not allowed to show themselves before others, yet it is important that in this space we are honest about who this person truly is...every aspect of her. Her hopes and dreams as well as her fears and doubts, because no one is perfect and fear is a matter of life. We must learn to be open and vulnerable and if we cannot do that with ourselves, than who can we do so with?

Next, is the person that God sees. Why is this important? Well, as much as we see ourselves, we must learn who God says we are as He created us. As we learn to reconnect with our God-given identity, we also learn to reconnect with our God-given purpose which helps us to move out of endless cycles. This also keeps us from attempting to "create," make-shift, or manifest our life as we learn who God is to and for us. Here is where we begin to realign ourselves with who He says we are and how he calls us, thus reconnecting with true power and authority. No longer seeking false connections and idols for our identity and destiny.

With God, we establish a firm foundation on which life is built and everything He does withstands time.

> "The King is enthralled by your beauty; honor him, for he is your lord."
> (Psalm 45:11)

Inner Work Exercise

Reflection Exercise:
Here we will dig deep into what you believe about yourself and why?

Instructions:
- Spend **time reflecting** on the following prompt.
- Write a page for to respond to the prompt. Push yourself to write a full page
- It is important to schedule time in your day to do the exercise so you are intentional with your time. Recommend placing it on your schedule and setting an alarm to ensure you have adequate time to write and reflect without being disturbed.

> "For I know the plans I have for you," declares the Lord, "plans to prosper you and not to harm you, plans to give you hope and a future."
> (Jeremiah 29:11)

Journaling Prompt #1

Describe yourself:
Time to take a look at who you are? This is _____ as a person. What do you like, what do you believe, what are your ambitions, and why? Look at your life...look at yourself in a mirror, and who and what do you see? Tell me who you see and why? DIG and be honest! This is not a time for superficial flowery stuff. How do you REALLY see yourself?

How God Sees you

Part 2: How does God see you?

Review the scriptures that express how GOD sees you. As you discover, read, and meditate on each text, do the following:

- Describe what you understand God is saying and why this is important. (*Choose* **five** *of the following 20*)

- Express what challenges you have (if any) with seeing yourself in this way and why? Where does this barrier stem from? Who and what circumstances facilitated your belief in seeing yourself differently or from moving the way that God sees you in this way? (**choose five**)

> "God is within her, she will not fall; God will help her at break of day."
> (Psalm 46:5)

WHAT GOD SAYS CONCERNING YOU...

1. I AM LOVED

"But because of his great love for us, God, who is rich in mercy made us alive with Christ even when we were dead in transgressions - it is by grace you have been saved." (Ephesians 2:4-5)

2. I AM A MASTERPIECE

"For we are God's worksmanship, created in Christ Jesus to do goodworks, which God prepared in advance for us to do." (Ephesians 2:10)

WHAT GOD SAYS CONCERNING YOU...

3. I AM CHOSEN

"For he chose us in him before the creation of the world to be holy and blameless in his sight." (Ephesians 1:4)

4. I AM FORGIVEN

"In him we have redemption through his blood, the forgiveness of sins, in accordance with the riches of God's grace." (Ephesians 1:7)

WHAT GOD SAYS CONCERNING YOU...

5. I AM A CHILD OF THE KING

"In love he predestined us for adoption to sonship through Jesus Christ, in accordance with his pleasure and will - to the praise of his glorious grace, which he has freely given us in the One he loves." (Ephesians 1:4-6)

6. I AM AN HEIR OF GOD

The wonder of it! Your inheritance, as God's child, is His kingdom and everlasting life in which to enjoy it with Him. (Matthew 25:34, Titus 3:7)

WHAT GOD SAYS CONCERNING YOU...

7. I AM MORE THAN A CONQUEROR

"Yet in all things we are more than conquerors through Him who loved us." (Romans 8:37)

8. I AM GOD'S TEMPLE

"Do you not know that you are the temple of God and that the Spirit of God dwells in you?" (1 Corinthians 3:16)

WHAT GOD SAYS CONCERNING YOU...

9. I AM VICTORIOUS

"But thanks be to God, who gives us the victory through our Lord Jesus Christ." (1 Corithians 15:57)

10. I AM NOT CONDEMNED

"There is therefore now no condemnation to those who are in Christ Jesus, who do not walk according to the flesh, but according to the Spirit." (Romans 8:1)

WHAT GOD SAYS CONCERNING YOU...

11. I AM GUARDED BY GOD'S PEACE

"And the peace of God, which surpasses all understanding, will guard your hearts and your minds through Christ Jesus." (Philippeans 4:7)

12. I AM ACCEPTED

"Therefore, accept each other just as Christ accepted you so that God will be given glory." (Romans 15:7)

WHAT GOD SAYS CONCERNING YOU...

13. I AM HEALED

"O Lord my God, I cried to you for help, and you have healed me." (Psalm 30:2)

14. I AM SURROUNDED BY GOD'S MERCY

"Many sorrows shall be to the wicked; But he who trusts in the Lord, mercy shall surround him." (Psalm 32:10)

WHAT GOD SAYS CONCERNING YOU...

15. I AM BEAUTIFUL

"You are altogether beautiful, my love: there is no flaw in you."
(Song of Solomon 4:7)

16. I AM NOT ALONE

"Fear not, for I am with you; Be not dismayed, for I am your God. I will strengthen you, Yes, I will help you, I will uphold you with my righteous hand." (Isaiah 41:10)

WHAT GOD SAYS CONCERNING YOU...

17. I AM SUFFICIENT

"Not that we are sufficient of ourselves to think of anything as being from ourselves but our sufficiency is from God." (2 Corinthians 3:5)

18. I AM STRONG

"Therefore I take pleasure in infirmities, in reproaches, in needs, in persecutions, in distresses, for Christ's sake. For when I am weak, then I am strong." (2 Corithians 12:10)

WHAT GOD SAYS CONCERNING YOU...

19. I AM BLESSED

"Blessed are those who dwell in Your house; They will still be praising You." (Psalm 84:4)

20. I AM HOPEFUL

"For I know the thoughts that I think toward you, says the Lord, thoughts of peace and not of evil, to give you a future and a hope." (Jeremiah 29:11)

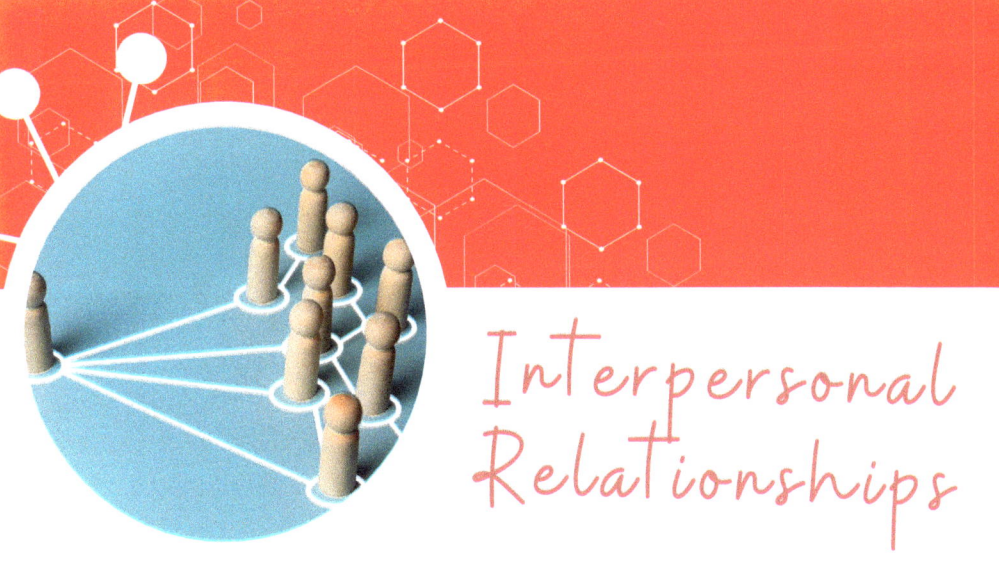

Interpersonal Relationships

Part 3. How others see you

Do you expect or want others to see you the way God sees you, yet you have trouble seeing yourself this way? Do you NEED others to validate these qualities about you in order for you to accept yourself in this way? Again, this is the time to DIG DEEP and have a serious talk with yourself. A soul-searching moment. What happens when others do not see you in this way? What implications does it have on your overall well-being and outlook on life and your future?

> "Charm is deceptive, and beauty is fleeting; but a woman who fears the Lord is to be praised."
> (Proverbs 31:30)

REFLECTION EXERCISE
INTERPERSONAL RELATIONSHIPS

REFLECTING ON HOW OTHERS SEE YOU AND THE IMPACT IT HAS ON YOUR INNER WELL-BEING

Do you expect or want others to see you the way God sees you, yet you have trouble seeing yourself this way?

Do you NEED others to validate these qualities about you in order for you to accept yourself in this way?

What happens when others do not see you in this way?

What implications does it have on your overall well-being and outlook on life and your future?

03
THE FUTURE YOU

This is where we begin taking a turn and shifting to connecting to the future you desire. With a breakthrough in accepting who you are according to God, your Creator, you can begin to move with the purpose and plans he has for you. So, let's start exploring these.

Dreams!

Background: Dreams - As a child possibilities were endless and the world was your oyster. You thought you could do anything and had th wildest and most daring dreams. Unfortunately, life and people happened. Circumstances and situations came along and seemed to snuff out the possibility of those dreams ever happening.

For some, you worked extremely hard to hold tight to those dreams and working tirelessly to make them come true to no avail. Seems there were times you go so close you could even feel or see it, all to just feel like it got further away from you.

But here's the deal. God gave you those dreams and he would not give them to you for nothing. The key is to understand how to move with Him, according to who he is, his word and what he says concerning you.

As we mature, not just physically but emotionally and spiritually realigning ourselves with God we get to rediscover those dreams but this time seeing them through a new perspective. This time we begin to understand how he gave us something that will help others as he is glorified.

Let's take a new look at our dreams to see how we will work with God so that he maybe glorified. Then in return, we shall be blessed to be a blessing.

> "Do not be conformed to the pattern of this world, but be transformed by the renewing of your mind."
> (Romans 12:2)

Looking Back

One of our first steps in reconnecting with previous dreams is deciphering between human desires and divine communication.

We tend to get frustrated with why dreams are not manifesting the way we thought they should, based on old dreams.

Here are a few key things we need to remember when it comes to dreams:
- Biblical Significance and Interpretation
- Connection with desires
- Processing, consolidation, reconciliation

"I can do all this through him who gives me strength."
(Philippians 4:13)

Bible Significance & Interpretation

The Bible gives several references to provide insights relating to dreams. We learn that dreams are used in multiple ways: Divine communication, Symbolism, Warning/Instruction, Testing/confirmation, and there are even Deceptive Dreams.

Without proper caution and a deeper understanding of biblical context, we can be led astray when interpreting the meaning of a dream. Furthermore, we have to take into account many variables concerning dreams, such as the circumstances the person is facing, their culture, and the overall teachings of scripture. Oh, and let's not forget their relationship with God. This is why interpretation is not taken lightly, and connecting with the right help for wisdom and understanding will aid in anchoring us in realistic expectations of our dreams, the information being spoken through them

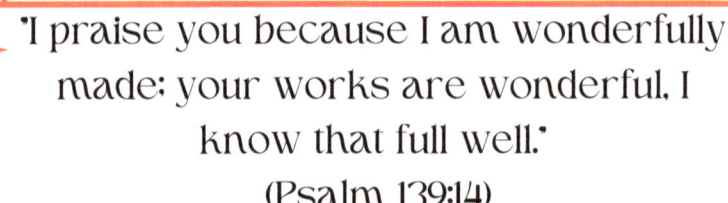

"I praise you because I am wonderfully made; your works are wonderful, I know that full well."
(Psalm 139:14)

Journaling Prompt #1

When you were FREE to believe that all things were possible, what did you dream of doing with your life?

Connection and Desires

As we gain new life experiences, these experiences can have a significant impact on influencing our desires, wishes, and aspirations. Through our dreams, we have the opportunity to manifest our deepest desires, the unconscious desires that may not be recognized or acknowledged in waking life. The desires that are suppressed or hidden can be due to fear or even trauma. In fact, for some, dealing with or highlighting conflict (or exploring clarification of possibilities) may be a person lands with dreaming.

The point is dreams are not always a direct interpretation of conscious desires. They are influenced by emotions, memories, experiences, and external stimuli. Having a professional or someone with special skills to aid you on this journey is vital.

> "And we know that in all things God works for the good of those who love him, who have been called according to his purpose." (Romans 8:28)

Journaling Prompt #2

Why did you stop dreaming or believing these things were possible? Do these dreams still somewhat linger in your thoughts? How have they changed or evolved?

_____

Processing, Consolidation, Reconciliation

Dreams have been known to be a source of inspiration, stimulating creativity and generating innovative ideas by accessing unconventional connections and associations in the mind. Dreams provide a unique platform for exploring new perspectives and gaining insight into various aspects of life, such as revealing hidden desires, fears, conflicts, and unresolved issues that may not be immediately apparent in waking life. Our dreams can help us with problem-solving and decision-making, as some people are able to reconcile conflicting emotions and promote a sense of wholeness and harmony within themselves.

While dreams vary from person to person, the key is to understand that dreams can provide personal meaning and significance that, when properly unlocked, can aid us in making important life decisions and evaluating one's well-being.

> "I am fearfully and wonderfully made: your works are wonderful. I know that full well."
> (Psalm 139:14)

Journaling Prompt #3

What are you doing that is different from what you dreamed, and why?

04
A NEWFOUND FAITH

This is where we begin taking a turn and shifting to connecting to the future you desire. With a breakthrough in accepting who you are according to God, your Creator, you can begin to move with the purpose and plans he has for you. So, let's start exploring these.

The way forward

In every journey, we reach axis points; in these axis points, we are forced to make decisions that determine the remainder of our journey and the outcome.

God will give axis points at 45, 90, 180, and 360 days which are review or evaluation periods. Therefore, establishing them here would be a great idea to ensure you are on track or in alignment with the plan(s) set forth by The Holy and Matchless One.

> "The Lord is my strength and my shield; my heart trusts in him, and he helps me."
> (Psalm 28:7)

The way forward

We will explore new ways of moving with God in your life as you begin to see yourself and the world around you in a new light!

Instructions: With what God has shown you, what shall you choose to do? We expect much from God, but what can He expect from you from this point on? Will you stop here or continue on this journey to deepen your relationship with Him? Most importantly, how will you do so? What will be your commitment?

> "For I am convinced that neither death nor life, neither angels nor demons, neither the present nor the future, nor any powers, neither height nor depth nor anything else in all creation, will be able to separate us from the love of God that is in Christ Jesus our Lord."
> (Romans 8:38-39)

Journaling Space

05
SELF-PRESERVATION

In the art of self-preservation, we must learn to properly care for ourselves, whom God says we are, what He has placed in us, and provide for us.

Self-preservation is commonly thought of as self-care, but when we think of self-care, we often solely refer to things like spa days, treating ourselves to things, or even "checking out" for a much-needed mental health day. There is much more involved as we must learn to protect our peace, hope, and even our faith to prevent us from falling off course, losing ourselves, and losing the desire to accomplish or achieve our God-given dreams and purpose.

Self-preservation teaches us how to fight rightfully!

You are a Warrior!

Did you know being lauded as a woman warrior is noble and honorable, yet to be known as fierce is not? Today, we have taken on terms to mix in with the current culture, yet we must be mindful of what we say about ourselves.

In the bible, fierce meant violent, outrageous, not restrained. Even the English definition immediately refers to the word as marked by extreme and violent energy before defining it as strong and powerful. The key is to understand that is not a positive trait to identify as, especially as we have learned that we received our identity from God. Remember, we are made in the image of and likeness of him; therefore, understanding who and what we say about ourselves should reflect who he is.

Let's take a new look at our dreams to see how we will work with God so that he may be glorified. Then in return, we shall be blessed to be a blessing.

The term warrior is more commonly used biblically and for God. Warriors such as Deborah were fearless and obedient to God.

Keeping this in mind, we learn how to prepare ourselves for battle when the time comes.

> "The Lord is my strength and my shield; my heart trusts in him, and he helps me."
> (Psalm 28:7)

You are a Warrior!

There are times we must fight to preserve who we are, what God says concerning us, and what He has for us.

Use these three keys in the art of fighting properly:

- **Defensive vs. offensive** - We get offended when people say things we do not like. Stop! Why are you allowing people to throw you off course when you know the truth about who you are and what you are about? Why are you spending time defending yourself before foolish people rather than using that time to pursue what God has placed in you wisely?

- **Standing your ground** - Stop allowing others to take what God has given you. God has given you peace, love, joy, and a sound mind, so why are you giving that away to anyone who comes to steal it from you? They can't take it unless you give it to them.

- **Speaking up** - Learn to use the voice God has given you. Speak up for yourself. Advocate for yourself to others and to God. Prayer is powerful, so use it appropriately. Stop waiting and asking others to pray for you and pray for yourself. Stop crying when others do not step in and speak up for you...do it for yourself.

> "The Lord is my strength and my shield; my heart trusts in him, and he helps me."
> (Psalm 28:7)

Reflection Exercise

In what ways can you begin to properly preserve who you are and what God has placed in you?

Make this personal, thinking about what you do and what you must change. This will help you maintain accountability as you dig deep!

06
ART OF GRATITUDE

Art of Gratitude is a powerful practice that can greatly enhance one's life. It involves acknowledging and appreciating the things we have, both big and small. By focusing on what we are grateful for, we shift our perspective from one of lack to one of abundance. This can lead to increased happiness, improved relationships, and a more positive outlook on life. In order to cultivate gratitude, it can be helpful to keep a gratitude journal, reflect on the good things that happen each day, and express appreciation to others. With consistent practice, gratitude can become a way of life that brings joy and fulfillment.

Giving Thanks where Thanks is due!

Learning to love yourself also includes shifting your relationship with God. One way is learning to show gratitude to God through all circumstances, as this has the power to transform our personal lives.

Too often, we tend to show gratitude to God when we receive things, yet we should understand that showing gratitude means doing so at all times and every time.

When we understand and practice this art of gratitude, our perspective shifts, it cultivates contentment, enhances joy, builds trust and faith, and cultivates humility and emotional well-being.

When we express gratitude to God, we create a space for His presence and blessings to flow in our lives. Gratitude transforms our perspectives, emotions, and actions. It is a catalyst for personal growth and spiritual transformation and a life filled with abundant blessings.

As you think about your transformation and process your thoughts for moving forward, how can you begin to express gratitude to God?

For this next exercise, spend time reflecting on your Gratitude to God and write your prayer of gratitude.

> "Always give thanks to God the Father for everything, in the name of our Lord Jesus Christ.
> (Ephesians 5:20)

Journaling Prompt

Journaling Prompt

TRAITS OF A STRONG WOMAN

She is courageous

She knows who she is

She builds up others

She doesn't see showing emotions as a weakness

She follows her intuitions and doesn't overthink everything

She is truly happy and knows what it takes to make her own happiness

She owns her successes and believes in herself

She does not let the opinions of others influence her

She doesn't feel bad about breaking societal rules or reinventing herself

She continually works on being a better stronger strong woman

SCHEDULE YOUR COACHING CALL

Let's continue your journey towards discoverin your true identity and purpose with a personalized strategy session. Together, we wi work out a plan that will put you on the right track to achieving your goals.

HELLO@SHAWANDARANDOLPH.COM

SHAWANDARANDOLPH.COM | LEARNING TO LOVE YOURSELF, AGAIN

www.ingramcontent.com/pod-product-compliance
Lightning Source LLC
Chambersburg PA
CBHW061752070526
44585CB00025B/2867